Compte Goshorne, John Wallace Josh-Horn

Hints from the Hornograph on the Signs of the Times

Or, the unsealing of the hermetic books of Joseph the Hebrew

Compte Goshorne, John Wallace Josh-Horn

Hints from the Hornograph on the Signs of the Times
Or, the unsealing of the hermetic books of Joseph the Hebrew

ISBN/EAN: 9783337318239

Printed in Europe, USA, Canada, Australia, Japan

Cover: Foto ©Lupo / pixelio.de

More available books at **www.hansebooks.com**

HINTS

FROM THE

HORNOGRAPH

ON THE

SIGNS OF THE TIMES

OR THE

UNSEALING OF THE "HERMETIC BOOKS" OF

JOSEPH THE HEBREW.

" Of Haran Are We!"

DR. COMPTE GOSHORNE, C. P.

MINISTER-GENERAL

N. C. E.

HORNHOME PUBLICATIONS:

PHILADELPHIA.

1879.

TO My Church! My Valentine! *TWO BOOKS!*

GO FORTH!

Ye Twin Sons of Joseph,

To do the Work of Your Father HERMES,

And without any other *Preface* than

"OF HARAN ARE WE!"

Or any other Apology for Your Existence

than to Teach the Law as it was taught to Moses,

In whose Son You Live as GERSHON, "a Stranger here,"

But whose Higher Lineage is From

SALEM'S PROPHET KING!

And if the World call you "Mysterious," or a

Subtile Agent, tell them that *Mercury* was ever thus,

And that You seek "A Peculiar People!"

That You may Lead a SECOND Restoration, as

SALATHIEL did the *FIRST!*

Who gives a Sceptre to a "Sister's Son!"

He'll *take it* when he's need of one!

—*New Salic Law.*

CANTERBURY HALL,
FEB. 14th, 1879.

Entered According to Act of Congress, by the Author, in the Year 1878, being the Five Thousand Six Hundred and Thirty-Eighth of the Jewish Era, and of the Restoration of Israel the First.

Note. — NO ONE has been empowered by the Author to use the HORNOGRAPH (" *Urim*") nor has the secret of its operation been communicated to any one, neither can it be except by transmission through Aaron's (Haran's) Line.

COMPTE GOSHORNE.

Office of the HORNHOME PUBLICATIONS, No. 4 North 13th St.

PHILADELPHIA.

INTRODUCTION.

THE TRANSIT SCALE.

A VIEW OF THE PRINCIPAL PLANETARY CONJUNCTIONS, AND
REVOLUTIONS IN THE CELESTIAL WORLD AFFECTING THE DES-
TINIES OF ISRAEL.

Calculated by the Chaldean *Saros*, or the conjunction of Solar
and Lunar Measures of Time.

As also from the Earth's shifting Magnetic Centre as the *Lode-
Star* of Israel's Migrations, and its present position as deter-
mined by the Star *Regulus* and its relation to the Earth in the
great planetary Re-union of 1881.

The *Interior* Planets or those of particular interest and impor-
tance in all Historico-Chronological Calculations, as also in the
fuller *Prophetic* or Metronomic Scale, may be correlated as follows:—

Transits of Mercury at intervals of 3, 7, 11, and 46 years.

Transits of Venus at intervals of 8, and 235 years.

Seven *principal* Transits of Mercury equal to one of Venus.

Multiples of these according to a Method unused since the
building of the Great Pyramid, and too minute and comprehen-
sive for insertion here will in due time startle the Scientific
world with a Revelation of some things in regard to the Antiquity of *Civilization* upon this planet which they as yet have
scarcely dreamed her to be in possession of! But to the end
that the Church and the World may be edified *a little, even now,*
before the 8-fold chord of the New Æon of 1881 is struck, the
following "Hint" may be deemed as not without its value.

The Moon passes through the 12 Terrestrial Signs once every
month.

The Sun is posited in each of the Celestial Signs (or divisions
of the heavens) once every year.

12 Revolutions of the Moon concentric, ("wheel within wheel") are equal to one of the Sun. The Unit of Measure.

12 Revolutions of the Sun equal to 144 of the Moon.

1000 Revolutions of the Sun, or *Earth*, equals 12,000 of the Moon: or 12,000 Lunations in 1000 years,—the Cyclic Node,— and in 12,000 years or 144,000 Lunations, the Cyclic-Encyclic *Arc*, the 12 times 12,000 of the "dispersed of Israel" *still jour-neying in the flesh*, are Restored by Hypostatic Union with the *New Church Episcopal*, which though *localized* by the Magnetic Meridian to the Prophetic site of the

"CHURCH IN PHILADELPHIA"
(St. John's, Rev. 3:7),

Yet is present to the thought of its Minister-General (*Thoth, or Hermes*) wherever the name of God is spoken!

—If I go to the Mountains the "Hornograph" (Aaron'o-graph) will reveal her doings; If I encamp by the Sea her cry for the Word of Life will not be unheard! If I journey be-yond the Great Waters, or if in the hour of peril from her ene-mies she call unto me from the uttermost parts of the earth, there shall the Mercurial messenger be present with his aid, and to chain the lightnings of heaven as the ministers of his wrath!

The Noviciate in this the beginning of mysteries is cautioned not to confound the New Church Episcopal with the so-called Reformed Episcopal *travesty*, "or the deeds of the Nichol-sons, *which I hate!*" (Rev. 2 : 15)

"Ebal and Gerizim" O Israel! are now to thee instead of the Law and the Prophets: the *son of Gershom* (Jeshurun), Gozan, or Goshen, is still among you,—but what of the Scribes and Pharisees which *sit in Moses' seat!* I do not know that in measuring out the "curses of Ebal" I do justice to the expecta-tion of that "V. D. M." who at his coming was to "curse and swear, and stamp with his feet!" but I mouth it as well as I can,—*and I am shod with brass!*

THE "*BACK-SLIDE*" TRANSIT SCALE.

Babylon the Great, Is Fallen! Is Fallen!"

Rev. 14 : 8.

Collateral with the line of Israel's developement towards her predestined glory in the latter day, is the line of the Dragon, or the "man of 66," or of *six-hundred* three-score and six, and the continuation of whose empire is *calculated* both by Daniel and John the Revelator, and in exact accordance with the secret or Hermetic *nexus* of the Saronic Cycle; and which may be stated for future explanation somewhat as follows:

HERMETIC CYPHER:

A LION

470

627

A BEAR 470   627   627   470 A LEOPARD

△

470

A DRAGON

NEXUS:

See Page 14, or *Adamic Cycle.*

4 □ 3 & 5.,—or 12, the trine and square, or 1881.

609 by trine 1827 (*nexus*) G & K plus 50–4 1877 [G. W.] 1881.

Line of the WORD. (12th Æon).

A. M. 5625 = 1875 A. D. △ (3) or the Jewish Era, —10.

1875 X 2 or 3750, B. C., the Abrahamic *Era.*

—1875, or the *Last Coil of the Dragon. Out,* 1875—'81.

ADAM is schooled by *Atlas* (Adon) 375 years before he was constituted or created "head" of the race, as Abraham through Melchizedek, the *second Adon* (Ich Dien!) was for *a like period* indoctrinated into all the mysteries of Egyptian *servitude* before in the Children of Jacob his eyes should behold the land of *Canaan*, that *blessed offspring* of Noah's younger son, the inventor of Letters, the originator of Arts and Sciences, and whose claim to the respect of all the Caucasian race is fitly described on Page 65, of the *HORNBOOK*.

This 1875 years period then, contains the *connecting link* of all the historic and *pre*-historic Ages of the World, and may be divided and sub-divided until is found the *measuring-line* of the Prophets and the fate of the world's overshadowing *BABEL* stands disclosed!

11,250 A. M. (*initial*), 9,375—7,500—5625—3750—1875.
1875—750 X 2——375 X 2——750 X 2 1875.
By Fractions, 1881.

Which *to him who hath understanding* Rev. (13 : 18) contains the secret of the "time, times, and the dividing of times" (Dan. 12 : 7.) and while sounding the Great Jubilee Call of the Restoration of Israel wields the iconoclastic blow of *Time* at the feet of Daniel's Colossal Image of Empire!

As the North Pole of the Earth now inclines toward the first degree of *Cancer* we complete one great cycle of the celestial sphere, and begin to *go backward* for a new round upon the *dial of the Ages!* and as the *Hermetic links* are caught up in the "warp and woof" of History *Babel* grows weak, her speech incoherent, her knees begin to totter! *and ROME PREPARES TO FALL!*

Israel *was planted*, or the Holy Seed scattered abroad by their several captivities, about the year 625 B. C., when the Kingdom of Babylon was in its glory, and the Children of the Promise were seeing their darkest days. *This was that Head of Gold.*

625 years more, and Babylon was still powerful enough *as Rome* to foster the greatest superstition of Reformed heathenism that the world ever witnessed, and by force of arms to cherish the Line of *the Keys* (burglarious) for 600 years longer, when the sword of Mahomet put an end to their power in the East

and drove her aspiring and relentless hordes Westward to perish in the path of Civilization! *This was her Arms and Breast of Silver.*

625 years more, and the *Haranian* Crest of King John of Bohemia bowed beneath the stroke of Edward the *Black Prince*, and the secret lineage of the "Horn-Child" (Corsican, *Kyrnois,* or Caranus) was transferred to England, and the motto of that Alexandrian Crest three ostrich-feathers, with the inscription in German "Ich Dien!" (Adon) *I Serve!* became the possession of the Prince of Wales—about the same time that the *curse of Conquest* or the Crusades had filled the throat of an "open" Sepulchre at Jerusalem with the bodies of about 600,000 *fools*—and the Great Plague had infected and carried off about "a third part" of the inhabitants of Europe and the East,—while about the same time the Ancient stream of Learning was beginning to rise from its submergement under the Babylon rubbish of the Ages, and the foundations of English Literature, English Church, and Anglo-Saxon Israelitish Penn-Charter American Liberty were being laid! This was that "belly and thighs of brass" *badly damn-aged!*

Six hundred and twenty-five years more and the work of Papal (Babel?) disintegration has reached the "feet" of the image, already but an adulteration of iron with clay, and as the Head of the New Church Episcopal rises above that latest development of religious sensationalism, the *Reformed* Episcopal *Tail of the Dragon* methinks I hear a Voice from out the dim Prophetic Past reminding them (if they would but hear!) that they cannot *reform an Ethiopian,* or a leopard, but to leave the Restoration of Israel to him "who maketh all things New" even to the *triple crown,* or the NEW TIARA, of which the heir to the Principality of "New Wales" may in his next Volume deign to speak!

PRIMORDIAL GENESIS.

CHAPTER I.

IN THE BEGINNING

A	WILL"	Z
ay!	*Volis*	zeal, (*seal*)
or, 'Yes'	or, Æolus	'But'
Essence of Light,	Spirit, or Breath	begat *Why*
or, *Od*, begat	begat	Y
B	Scintilla	or, *division*,
or, 'be'	and Scintilla begat	and 'why'
existence,	Radialis	begat
of *Volis*,	and Radialis	X
Will,	begat *Lux*,	or *cross-*
whose fiat *Go, Od!*	Light,	*purposes* or
or, Radialis,	and Lux	'cross-wills'
'the Good'	begat	or, WW
begat	Ephemeris	a duality in
the Positive	and	Nature
or 'creative' force,	Ephemeris	from the *Nay!*
Light,	or *Day*	or *increative*
of Ges, the *Earth*	begat	voice of matter
the	Chronos	against *Yea!*
Negative element	the *Earth-born*	the positive or
opposing the birth	'Son-of-Light'	Odyllic force
of Abel,	who begat	which says
the originator	*JEUD*	Be! or Exist!
or preserver, the	and Jeud begat	in spite of *No!*
the Positive	Atlantis	or Darkness which
Creative Force or	and Atlas begat	begat Cain,
Animus,	Arun of Geesh, or	the 'worker'
Soul of	Gesh-'Arun	contriver,
the World.	(Jeshurun)	or opposer,

Or,

JESU AARON,

who constituted, or *'created'*
Adam head of the race on the Sixth
Day of CREATIVE EVOLUTION, and
Adam begat Cain and Abel at the Sixth of the world's
12,000 year stages, or the Eleventh of her 6,000 year stages.
And this is the Stone, or Diamond, which was "cut out
of the mountain without hands" and in the
spirit and power of *Eliakim* began
the sixth Adamic resurrection to be consum-
mated 1881.

* *
*

Now Cain was the natural, Abel the spiritual son. Abel per-
sonated the higher moral and intellectual life of the race, as the
creator, originator, Cain was the imitator or fabricator who followed in his footsteps. So that when the evil principle of the
superiority of matter over its essential life principle insinuated
itself into the heart of Cain it caused a separation or antagonism
between the creative and the imitative in the constitution of man,
in consequence of which the material rose above the spiritual, or
Cain rose and killed his brother.

Cain was the first-born, of coarser make, and physically supe-
rior (by the help of a club) to his younger brother, as the spiritual is ever more refined than the material. The design of the All-
Wise Creator was by His breath infused through Abel to raise
and spiritualize the natural man, or Cain, but physical force tri-
umphed, the old and crude material refused to be so transmuted,
and transfigured, and the life of Abel was crushed. Did it leave
the human race then? no, for Seth was put in the place of Abel
as a factor of humanity more physically able to cope with the
line of Cain, while the line of Abel thus strengthened by this
bond of union with the *intermediate race* not only sustained a
physical status in the line of physical progress of that mediate
race but preserved the line of its *spiritual* genealogy unbroken
through sixty centuries of conflict with the incarnate powers of
darkness, or the inherent malignity of matter, and is now intin-

itely stronger and more enduring at this the beginning of a new
Era of Light than in any of the all but immeasurable cycles of
the Past.

Now we propose to trace the course of these inharmonious factors or elements of the human race from their first separation into antagonistic principles in the sons of the first *representative* human pair, and by genealogical and racial embodiment and developement all the way down the line of the ages until the present
time; believing that herein is the solution of that gigantic prob-
lem of human existence and destiny, the misunderstanding of
which lies at the bottom of all our National difficulties, as well
as of all the other nations of the world which are now in that
state of general fermentation that precedes all great political, to
say nothing of social and ecclesiastical revolutions.

Who then is the wise man but he who listens to the teachings
of Nature, buried deep in whose varied forms and manifestations
is the living God, that divine essence or substratum of things
external and material which remains unchanged and unchange-
able from the dimness of the remotest ages down through all the
cycles of eternity; the emanations of whose breath or essence is
Abel, or the spirit of man and that which it animates is *Cain*, or
the adversary, that *which was but is not* when man is once more
transformed into a spiritually developed being *more than* at the
first and the crude elements of his body return to the dust of
chaos, ere the spirit of creation brooded upon, or in it, to mould
it into the uses of the higher life!

CHAPTER II.
THROUGH ALL THE WORLDS!
KOH-I-NOR,
or *Light in Darkness*
begat
ZOROASTER,

Or *Life from a Star!* (pseudonym for *Jeshurun*), who took to himself *Scintilla*, daughter of Aldebaran, his 'Uncle,' and reproduced himself in all the starry worlds which compose the body of the All or Universal Father, until he reached the Heart, where re-celebrating his Millennial nuptials with Scintilla, the radiant Daughter of Aldebaran, or the Hyades he
begat another self,
or Son,

And sailed through Æther till he reached the Hand, where as Mercurial or Odyllic *Light* he began to create the world in which we live, ten thousand times ten thousand years from his own birth in th Æther All, and its central sun, till when a crystal Zoe, shot from that heart of hearts to meet Sciatilla in the depths of chaos where he
begat Lux
Prior to the
First Day of Creation,
And Lux begat Ephemeris *of* Etherialis, and Ephemeris
begat Chronos or Time
on the
Third Day of Creation,
Or, 33,000 years from "*Fiat lux!*"
And Chronos begat Jeud, who was sacrificed to the relentless
Saturn on that ever memorable
Fourth Day of Creation,

When Jupiter came to Venus, and the influence of these two planets were united for the developement of the Earth.

And Jupiter and Venus

begot the Atlantides

At the middle of the Jupiterian and the beginning of the Mars stage of earth's evolution or the

Fifth Day of Creation:

and Atlas and Atlantis

begat Adam and Eve

on the

Sixth Day of Creation,

When Koh-i-nor is reproduced in Abel, in the 60,000th year from 'Yohi yior!' or the fiat of *Volis*, Let there be light! though Day for *our* planet was yet unconstituted, its evolving mass of incandescent matter not having made the transit of the *timeless* void to have her future progress marked and pointed by the Dial of the Ages!

Now if you will consider that Man, *as man*, existed on this planet at least 66,000 years before the present or 60,000 years before the time of the last-mentioned Adam, or last point of re-incarnation, we will go on: and say that

As in the last Six Thousand years *the entire history of our planet has been repeated in epitome, we shall consider this period the Cycle within Cycle or "wheel within a wheel" understanding which we may radiate to the outermost bounds of the everlasting Kosmos: So true it is that that which was is that which shall be, and there is no new thing under the sun!*

Now as we do not propose at present to write a New *Genesis*, provided the Old can be plausibly interpreted, we proceed at once to a developement of the Hindian or Brahminic *Ages*, or Cycles of Time, *upon their later Jewish basis*, as being of more immediate interest, and resting upon historic data more accessible to the general reader.

That the Jewish National Church, or Theocracy, was developed from the older Hindian, and after its culminating, or centralization, became the source from which the later Hindian renewed the vigour of its youthful priority is one of the mysteries of re-incarnation on the larger or national scale which few modern theologians will have sagacity enough to discern, or when discerned, have honesty enough to admit. But until they do admit it they might as well hang their harps upon the willows, and be content with their Captivity in the meshes and superstitions of Babylon, while the ransomed believers in the spiritually and physically *regenerate* New Heavens and New Earth will heed the Millennial Call to the *Sabbath of Rest*, and go up to Zion with their harps strung to new songs from Lyra and the Pleiades on this the Fiftieth Jubilee (50 times 50 yrs.) from the Captivity, and from the Exodus the 66th Jubilee Return, and from the translation of Enoch, with his hosts of redeemed Atlantides, or Ancient Brahminic Spirits, the 99th.,—counting backwards from this the end of the Sixth, and beginning of the Seventh of the World's millenary stages, or the grand re-commencement of the Great Equinoxial Precession Year, or cycle of 25,000 common, or Solar years, the order and *rationale* of which we are now about to develope by the application of the Transit Scale.

NOTE.—In order to preserve as clearly as possible the orderly and consecutive arrangement of the several subjects and chapters of this work we cannot pause here for the purpose of conducting the reader through the full developement and application of the TRANSIT SCALE, but in this, and all subsequent allusions thereto, he will consider that reference is had to the Chapter, or Chapters especially devoted to the elucidation of that subject; leaving him in the majority of cases to make his own applications and draw his own conclusions, which is about all that could be expected in a series of "Hints,"—but if at any time *more* is given than a hint requires or the data seem to justify, let him possess his soul in patience until the further unrolling of the prophetic scroll justifies *all* the allusions of the Hornograph, *and a good many more which the weak hearts and perverted judgments of the Babylonians in our midst would at present hardly be able to bear!*

CHAPTER III.

THE FALL WHICH WAS A RISE.

At the first beginning of this last of the Six Thousand Year Cycles the line of separation between the descendants of Cain and of Abel, or the natural and spiritual elements of the human race, was so slightly marked that they named their off-spring by almost the same identical names from one generation to another, until the time of Lamech, the father of Noah, who had two wives, in which the two races were again united in his children, and Ham, the grandson of Lamech was made to bear the curse inflicted upon Cain to purify him from the evil principle which in the family of Noah survived the Deluge, and again became prevalent as an indirect consequence of the great Solar heats which devastated all the East about the time that the Pentateuch records the Fall of Man.

SETH	ABEL	CAIN.
Enos		Enoch
Cainan		
Mahalaleel		
Jared		Irad
Enoch		Mehujael
Methuselah		Methusael
LAMECH		LAMECH
Noah,		Noah.

—Or Ten generations in the Spiritual line corresponding to Seven in the Natural, which is the same proportion that we will find to exist between the two different genealogies of the God-Man of the Christians as given in the first chapter of the book of Matthew and the third chapter in that of Luke, and which two-fold Personage was an exact reproduction of the Adam Kadman of the Hebrew Kabbalists, and hence his claim to be considered the "Second Adam" is not without foundation, and his right to deification by Humanity was about as good as that of any person that ever lived.

GOD is the Lord and the Son-of-Man was His Prophet: Let him hear and understand who will!

Ham, or "the Hot," then, prevailed as the grand-son of Noah, out of whom came Nimrod the Hunter, Mizraim father of the Egyptians; Phut and the Caphtorim, the Philistines and all the host of the Canaanites, or *Cainites*, who held possession of the Land of Promise, not by right but by conquest and oppression of the line of Abel or Seth, who were as yet pilgrims and strangers in Chaldea and Egypt until the time that they should have strength to claim their own, and make a servant of servants the Cain-ites as was foretold by Noah to Canaan the unfortunately aspiring son of Ham.

This brings us to the inevitable conclusion that God allows the existence of Evil for a wise and beneficent purpose, and suffers it to prevail within certain fixed and definite limits for the fuller developement of the higher factors of human progress, and when these have reached a self-sustaining status, the principle of evil recoils upon itself like its symbol the serpent, and is its own destruction, while the spiritual nature of man released from its coil goes on progressing toward perfection, never again to return to the chrysalis from which it has been developed. It is the Psyche of the Greeks, the "Butter-fly" freed from the case in which it was matured, and hence the symbolical name and character of Butter-fly the symbol of the Soul and emblem of Immortality.

Thus Adam, the man of earth, was the case or chrysalis from which was evolved Abel the spiritual factor of the Race in its upward developement; in which *case* or under whose care Abel had been nurtured until he was able to cope with the world for a physical and spiritual existence. But the strength of the Adversary, who was the first-born and held supreme sway, crushed the bud of his spiritual existence, so that he was destined to remain another 6,000 years before he should have sufficient strength again to burst the chrysalis and manifest himself to the world a glorified and transfigured spirit, the winged Mercury, messenger of the gods, which all the powers of darkness could not chain,

nor the cerements which bound him prevail to keep him longer
enclosed.   The ship Argo has reached the end of the Milky-way,
the Churning of the Deep is over, the butter is made, the *serum*
or whey is left, which eating and drinking ye eat and drink the
the body and blood of righteous Abel, while his beautiful and
released spirit is the butter-fly which has flown from its earthly
tabernacle to other spheres, "And as often as ye do this" saith
the Spirit "do it in remembrance of Me!"

Chapter IV.

CHRONOLOGICAL.

Now if I choose to count time by commencing in the middle and radiating both ways, or by commencing at both ends and arriving in the middle, and thereby attain more satisfactory, and in every way more reliable results than by the ordinary method of selecting some point or other at random, and in spite of the cries and remonstrances of the outraged historians and sages of Antiquity, making *that* the "beginning of authentic history" I do not see but that my system of computation in cycles is its own justification, *and in need of no apology for sweeping all other methods out of existence!*

The fallacy of reckoning time *in a straight line* rather than in the orderly developement of progressive cycles is particularly fascinating to the partially educated historians of modern times, who, even supposing that they had at times, and during more lucid intervals of thought, dreamed of a better method, yet crushed the waking fancy of an immortal truth, lest perchance it might displease some crowned head or captious duke, or to subserve their own private aims at popularity and preferment at the expense of a reputation for veracity and sound judgment, if not with contemporaries, at least to the more candid mind of an enlightened posterity.

Shades of Usher, Lloyd, and Stillingfleet! What a Herculean task ye have left for somebody to do in after times, if only to reconcile your clashing and confused systems! Being compilers of incidents, names and dates, rather than historians, you failed to recognize the philosophy of history, and though you have thereby escaped the opposite fault of theorizing, and perhaps the temptation of spinning yarns for the distorted warp and woof of modern history manufacturers, yet do your skeletonian compilations of names and dates but exhale the fragrance of the dry-bones in the Valley of Jehoshaphat!

Wind then, O Gabriel, a Melchizedekian Cohorn resurrection blast! And as the myriads of the buried Past spring to new life in the persons of their Western-world descendants, let the "dry-bones" of Israel's History shuffle together with the restored notes of a lost harmony, and the now agitated plain of Armageddon's spiritual conflict teem with the waking millions of Israel's re-incarnate sons! And all those grand and noble pages of their all but Celestial history be read in the shifting hosts of the Stars of God, which from their Eastern vigils o'er Chaldaean plains have come to rest sublimely in the Zenith of the Foreshadowed Land! the Canaan of their hopes—the Western Land of Promise!

Before entering upon the *long periods* of history as developed by the Transit Scale, we will do what we can with the History of the World as it at present stands, or in other words endeavor to synchronize the different systems of chronology as relating to that history, which we have already termed in a previous chapter as simply the latest of the world's 6,000-year cycles or stages of developement; and as that has also been termed in the same connection an epitome or microcosm of all antecedent and subsequent cycles, so it must have a middle, or radiating point, and a circumference, and we, in accordance with the proposition already laid down at the opening of this chapter, will now select that centre or radiating-point and unfold the historic scroll *both ways* until it reaches the Eastern and Western bounds of civilization, as embracing the entirety of human destiny within its limits.

Wake, O Israel to the sublime truth of thy re-incarnation, or spiritual New-birth! All Nations are represented in thee: the Persians, and Medes, and Elamites of this great Fifty-times-Fifty Pentecostal Jubilee of the "dispersed of Israel" now camped upon American shores! And even the 'dwellers beyond the sea' —Kelts, Cambrians, Scotch-Irish, and English-Saxons, Hebrews of the Hebrides, and the Japhetic races of Iona and the Isle of Man! Greeks, Romans, and Hellenistic Jews! Orange-Nassau-renian, Vaudois, Kathari and Waldensian sleepers in the Alpine martyr-vales!—List to the bugle-blast of the Horn of Kyrnois, for the Lion of Judah sleeps no longer in the dust of St. Helena, and the Marsellaise is leading on his myrmidons to conscious victory!

Wake to the "Sun-burst of Erin," and to the now Æolian strains of Tara's forgotten Harp! which once upon the plains of Troy assembled the hosts of Hiram for the building of the Temple!—*and LYRA is our Zenith-star to-day!*

England now declines from her pristine glory, For "the sceptre *has departed* from Judah, and a law-giver from between his feet!"

Shiloh has come!

From Cycle to Cycle, or from Israel's Call to Israel's Restoration, three thousand seven hundred and fifty years!

From Cycle to Cycle, or from Adam's Fall to Esau's End, eighteen hundred and seventy-odd years!

From Adam "made" to Eden lost, three thousand seven hundred and fifty years!

At the end of the Old and the beginning of the New, "when Esau took hold upon the heel of Jacob" (Esdras.) was the dividing or "parting asunder of the times;" Memorialize *that*, O World! until we come to the "times and dividing of time" of the Prophet Daniel, and Saint John the Divine's most precisely calculated Astrological Revelations!

With this Hint, then, REST, O Historia's parti-colored Shades! The Stars are the Chroniclers of God!

Chapter V.

HISTOROLOGICAL.

The History of the Lost Tribes of Israel is the World's History in miniature. That proposition *stated* is that proposition *proved*. But the question may arise, Who *are* "the Israelites," and what is meant by the Restoration?

Mistaken notions exist with regard to the people called Israel, and the authenticity even of their Ancient history has not unfrequently been doubted.

There is a reason for this different from that "there is a reason for *all things* under the Sun!"

Israel has suffered both from her friends and her enemies. That has been the fate of all great principles and divinely inspired springs of human action.

It might have been ordered otherwise, but it *was* not.

It might naturally have been supposed then that at some time such a condition of things should cease to exist, and be replaced by a better. This is what the Prophets came to tell us and now they are vindicated.

The Prophets did not tell us all that they knew, nor are we to presume that they have told us much that they did not know; it is natural to suppose that they acted as other wise men would have done in like case: did the best they could according to the light that was given them.

"This is the Light that lighteneth all the World" except the denizens of Theological Seminaries.

We might have more light from the Prophets if these latter did not stand in the way.

They will not go in themselves, neither will they let others enter in to the New Jerusalem, that City of "Many Mansions."

When you find men inclined to look upon the light *and not see it*, you may conclude that blindness is their normal condition and that any undue anxiety after their spiritual welfare on the part of others might as well be postponed until the final judgment.

Let not this digression concerning Edom divert your thought from the line of Israel's unfolding destiny.

Edom is not confined to Theological Seminaries, nor is Israel all outside the Clerical profession.

Speaking of the Prophets, if we had even as much light as they we would have much clearer ideas of Inspiration than we have at present.

And when we get more light let us give *them* credit for what they have done in helping us thereto.

But since we are to have the substance of which they had only the shadow, let us feel doubly assured of the grounds of the Faith, in that as "others (they) have labored so we have entered into their labors."

WE are they because of their spirit which is in us. Hence *they* enjoy the fruits of their own labors, and *we* are those fruits. Man for man is the ancient Israel represented in the living souls of this Age and generation: They were the beginning of a Cycle of re-incarnation of which we are the End.

The seed had to be planted before it could grow, and after all its days and seasons of developement is it the *same*, or "some other kind of grain!"

Paul asked that question once but the conclusion was so evident that he did not stop to answer it.

His conclusion however might have been clarified by the contingent result of either an improved or debased product, but the same species.

Nature's organic forms and entities are Eternal but the types or moulds thereof are constantly changing.

"That which has been is that which shall be, and there is no new thing under the Sun."

A sensible History has a beginning, a middle, and an end.

A cause, an agent, and an effect.

A line, a point, and a circle.

A Nation has a beginning a centralization, and a decline.

A death, a beginning, and a culmination.

A Star has its rising, its meridian, and its setting.

And will repeat that cycle till rolling ages cease to move!

Just so many nations ever have or ever can exist upon this planet.   They are parts of one organic whole and if these do not return the Earth must needs mourn the loss of the human race.

If more should come she would not have room to contain them.

If even the Eastern Nations should come West our Sun-set-Land would not be able to contain them.

All things have their due proportion and of this we have had enough.

Turkey must stay where she is or be whipped.

And ere long must retreat to the high lands of Tartary or be trodden to dust in the Valley of Jehoshaphat and be sunken in the slime-pits of the Vale of Siddim.

She will not retreat.

ISRAEL MUST RETURN!

Chapter VI.

LOOK ON THESE STONES!

The *Jews* were a "peculiar people" and so were the Quakers who founded Philadelphia.

THEY did not found it but they prevented William Penn from doing so.

Philadelphia never was founded.

And if it was not founded then it is not a fit place to live in until it is.

It will be a fit place to live in.

When it is so William Penn will return.

That game of "Fox-and-Goose" has been nearly played.

Look on any Map of the Heavens for illustration while I proceed to deal with earthly things.

The Goose looks as if it had been Penn-ed, *pawned*, or trepanned *like the Three Balls on the Penn* "*Coat-of-Arms*," but what of the Fox!

The Goose is out of the Penn.

And had "Horns coming out of his hand."

Penn is no longer a Goose.

And will redeem that *pawn!*

"His horn has been exalted" at least above the measure of a goose.

"Go tell that Fox" (George) that he will be but a mouthful in the maw of the Unicorn!

That Herod must suffer for the Slaughter of the Innocents.

"My heart is inditing a good matter" And

With a quill of that plucking I will write the Fate of the City.

Which is that the Son of Penn shall return to his patrimony, or that his patrimony shall return to "him of the manor-born."

Restore him Penn-Square and you may keep the Manor.

Otherwise "not one stone shall be left upon another that shall not be thrown down."

Unless the City should become richer they are not likely even to be built up!

The City is in moderate circumstances.

The "Market-Place" *has been* thrown down!

If you build it up it will be thrown down again.

It is too near the Temple precincts.

Some *spires* and *steeples* were also thrown down, or twisted *into* their place, but that will not be noticed when we have a Church.

That was a stiff breeze when the "Sun-god" entered Scorpio on the 23rd. of October and flourished his "knotted cord" in that "Den of Thieves!"

Philadelphia will be more healthy.

That was a spiritual breeze,—fit precursor of the cleansing of the Temple courts.

The New Jerusalem will descend as soon as there is a place for it to 'light.

St. John the Divine promised Philadelphia a Church.—Rev. 3 : 7. And it would be a shame if she should be cheated out of it.

We will do what we can to cheat her into it.

Mercury was the "Lord of Thieves," otherwise he could not have out-witted them.

Some one tried to be Mercury and was crucified between two of his fellows.

He would have been crucified between "a dozen" but the rest "forsook him and fled."

The gods never die.

There is too much need of them to live.

Nor would *their* dying do *you* any good.

Your funeral expenses would not be any lighter.

LOOK ON THESE STONES!

✝✝✝✝✝✝ !☉! ✝✝✝✝✝✝

And then look up the title-deeds of the Penn property.

The Quakers are some of them good and some of them bad, in this respect they are like other people.

In some respects they are not like other people.

Their god is a "shad-belly" and their delight is in the rim of a hat.

Hat, Walk, and Conversation have a regard to that "cleanliness which is next to godliness" and that is about as near as they ever get to godliness.

And their front door-step is about as near as they ever get to cleanliness.

Eliakim Hicks did much to restore them to the wisdom of the righteous *Penn*, but they would none of him and cast him out of their synagogue.

Some few followed him and escaped from the falling timbers.

Philadelphia is becoming more healthy.

Death has become bond-holder to the possessors of ancient removed landmarks, but the spirit of *Fox* still inhabits their children.

But is not yet a fit place to live in.

"Lord, how long?"

Till the streets are cleaned and its walking carcases buried.

"Hark from the tombs a doleful sound!"

Like the Penn heirs they want what belongs to them and they are bound to have it!

Fear not, O Zadok-cee! "for there is no Resurection."

The spirits of dead men live in us both to judge and to be judged.

Here endeth the Iron Age and the breaking in pieces of the "iron-and-clay" in the feet of Daniel's Vision of Empire.

The stone that was "cut out of the Mountain without hands" has descended to become the Corner!

Which for the present is near the North-west Corner of Thirteenth and Market Streets.

Philadelphia is a fit place to live in.

And she is to have a Church, too! at least it was so written by John, Revelations 3. 7.

That "Church in Philadelphia" was a beautiful conception of John's and worthy of a great prophet!

His Astrological Foresight was unparalleled in the history of human ken, except perhaps the Ancients who were the models of his studies.

Newton and Kepler might have borrowed from him had not his system been too vast for their comprehension..

They had about as much idea of his Celestial Discourses as modern astronomers have of a Prophetic Church!

They reason to the end of their "knows" and pronounce the rest *unknowable.*

Their noses are of the Celestial *turn*, but brief.

When will ye learn wisdom O ye Star-gazers, and *Microscopists*? and when will ye have sufficient reflection to get understanding!

Perhaps that question might also be refered to the unknowable.

Philadelphia is lived in.

And she has her Church.

That bud in the wilderness shall blossom as the rose!

The Lillie of the Wol-ley's has not yet got out of her d'ab d'ess!

But she is as vain of her new-found glories as her High Cock-o-Lorum Lord-of-the-Walk! See Canticles, Book of

"And that glory she will not give to another!" See Heart Revelations in her private letters *when you find them.*

"My beloved is a garden enclosed , a spring shut up, a fountain sealed" the Daughter of Elizabeth, the Child of the Tudors, the Rose of Lancaster, the "Virgin Daughter of My People" re-born to an imperishable Crown when he that loveth mercy and executeth judgment shall appear *by the other door* of the Two-Door Line to declare that this stupendous joke of Creation is finished by the Lion of Judah carrying off his all-too-willing Bride! while those who in their pride, vain-glory and hypocrisy have been heedless of that Midnight Cry which was to herald the rising morn of the redemption of the world will be left an out-door standing comment on that no longer disputed reason why Jack didn't eat his supper!

Will the Lily of Israel now heed this, or is some mangy old Churchman still pouring into her ears, or rather those of her mother which are considerably larger and more receptive, his serpentine venom that the Son of Light is out at the elbows, that he can't pay his debts, or wouldn't if he could, that he is a gay deceiver, that he is a Lion in a lamb's skin, a Hercules in the garb of Adonis, an Adventist, a Millerite, a Ritualist, a Royalist, a Revolutionist, a believer in immortality and the final rectification of all things; a Jew, an Ephraimite, a strenuous advocate of Apostolic Succession in the line of 'Aaron but still more so as in the line of Salem's ancient Haran Kings, a believer that that which is is not that which always shall be, and various other things which in the eyes of the Devil would hardly be considered orthodox, and that consequently he is crazy and if allowed to run loose will make every sensible person think and act just as bad as himself!

A long story may be cut short when it has but one ending.

I want those "golden apples!"

Then LOOK ON THESE STONES! while I fling them at the head of the Old Dragon in the Garden of the Hesperides!

Philadelphia is a fit place to die in.

* * * * *　　　　* * * * *

The Graves of Greenwood are not so beautiful as the Laurel Hill Mansions of the Dead. *They* have not yet risen, but *here* their ghostly tenants walk about the streets.

They ask why William Penn was not buried among them that they might have rested more quietly till the final call.

He gave them the ground and they feel under obligations to him for providing for their temporal rest.

And seeing that they cannot find an inscription to him in all the winding mazes of the Schuylkill's white-flecked shores they have decamped to a less miasmatic region and live in the Celestial worlds around us.

They who have stones to their memories need no resurrection.
They are not obliged to walk the earth to keep alive the memory of their deeds.

LOOK ON THESE STONES!

And when the widow cries for bread will ye give them to—her husband!

Is there any taste in a block of marble, or will it say to the fatherless, Be fed and clothed!

Have you enough marble in Penn Square to finish that mighty structure?

Or would it pay *en masse* the City Debt!

Having furnished some poor men with work has it not done all the good that may be expected of it, or is it to stand a perpetual warning to the Nations!

In either case its destiny is fulfilled.

Then slip the halter of Judea's fate, and on the Lord's ground build a temple to the Lord.

And be sure first that the spiritual temple is complete before the natural is commenced.

LOOK ON THESE STONES!

And take them off that ground!

+
N
N
E
P
IAM
WILL-
TUDORS
PEMBROKE
JAMES PETER JOHN
ABRAM ISAAC JACOB
BRAHMA VISHNU SIVA
A B R A C A D A B R A

Chapter VII.

CALL TO THE "MANY MANSIONS."

ISRAEL was composed of the Twelve Tribes of the Human Race, and in close conjunction yet distinct from these were twelve others, which might be called barbarous or *inhuman*.

One Tribe for every Constellation (Zodiacal) and then a Double, or devil.

That "double" was their Shadow of Darkness to each, and these also were Tribes and Nations.

To those Doubles or Devils the Constellated Twelve were the Shadow of Light, and they hated them without a cause.

In an evil hour they drove them from their midst and were themselves swallowed up in Darkness.

*   *   *   *   * | *   *   *   *   *

Pharaoh and his hosts never forgot that lesson but are trying it again *on the spiritual plane.*

They would make you believe with Job's Friends that they are the people and that wisdom will die with them.

They would make you believe that there is no key to the Many Mansions, or that the writer of these Hints hasn't got it.

Either horn of the dilemma will answer their purpose of mystification provided one or the other be accepted.

They would make you believe that Israel was one narrow-minded, half-barbarous, one-idead "peculiar people," and not the acme of human civilization as the twelve representative tribes or nations of the Human Race.

They would make you believe that the stars do not shine, or if they do, that they cannot possibly have any influence upon man destiny.

They do not believe that 'one Star should differ from another Star in glory' unless the difference should be in favor of themselves.

What have we to say that the sentence of death should not be passed upon them!

Their Destiny has been made for them according to what they chose for themselves in the beginning, and if it is not now just what they would like to have it they have nobody to blame but themselves.

If they go to their devil it will be but in ratification of a previous contract.

It is not the principles involved but the consequences that they so much dread.

Many doubtless would not have so contracted had they not like Faust intended to cheat the devil in the end.

He is not so short-sighted in that which pertains to the perpetuity of his kingdom.

To blame God for what they have thus imposed upon themselves would be the heighth of absurdity.

Nevertheless some of them will persist in being *very absurd*.

"Who is this that cometh from Edom, with dyed garments from Bozrah" if it is not he whose coat of many colors had been dyed a deeper red in the blood of a "kid of the goats" by his cruel and perfidious brethren!

If Joseph had not been a better Brahmin than they were *Christna*-ians he would have cremated every mother's son of them as soon as they had arrived in Egypt.

But they had not yet filled up the measure of their iniquity and that of their fathers.

Until they had so done the pleasure of treading the winepress of the wrath of Almighty God would scarcely have been a sufficient inducement for leaving even for a time the honors and dignities of Pharaoh's Court.

He left them till the latter day that he might forgive them, and that those who would not accept forgiveness at his hands might be destroyed.

Now these make-believes want to *forgive Joseph* and write him the sinner instead of themselves.

This was a natural consequence of their belief in the doctrine of Vicarious Atonement.

Not even satisfied with the idea of of vicarious atonement they would fain make him a *vicarious sinner* in their stead.

So, doubtless, reasoned they who thought to make Joseph to die for their sins.

It is an ancient and much approved Doctrine for even Job's Friends had it.

And still, though the Book of Job is very ancient yet it is not as old as they concerning whom it was written.

"Fill up then the *immeasurable* iniquity of your fathers."

"He that hath an ear to hear let him hear what the Spirit saith unto the Churches."

XXXIX ARTICLES TOO MANY!

The "Divine Gift" or the secret of the application of the Hermetic Philosophy to the alleviation of suffering and the elevation of Humanity, was never *communicated* by the "laying on of hands;" but when disciples were sufficiently *indoctrinated*, that *seal of approbation* was the world's guarantee of their Apostleship.

Such gifts go forth from the Central 'OM or the Archi-Episcopate of Canterbury NEW, whose City within a city, as the "wheel within a wheel" shall ere long manifest the wisdom of the Divine Architect in the "lights and perfections" of *The Urim Hand*—that silent worker whose glorious New Salem City is the long-lost "Hornhome" (Air-h'ya'ne, *Eden*,) or the world's external (Masonic) manifestation of its *interior self*.

Ministers of suitable education and capacity may from time to time be——*If thou understandest not what thou readest please refer to Page M 49, of the HORNBOOK.*

Here beginneth the First Lesson.

The Clergy are requested to *turn over a New Leaf!*

RABBI BEN ISRAEL.

SCHOOL OF THE PROPHETS,
   PHILADELPHIA.

END OF BOOK FIRST.

OLD WORLD, FAREWELL!

"SELAH" DAY:

THE NEW SABBATH

OR THE

ASTRONOMICAL DAY OF "REST."

SUNDAY, 12 M. to MONDAY, 12 M.

SERVICES: (11th *Hour*) (Public), Monday, 10-30 to 12 M.
New Anglican Ritual.

SPECIAL: On Selah-Days nearest the *Equinoxes*, Great Transits, *principal Lunar changes*, and at such other times as may be
particularized in

THE NEW ASTRONOMICON:

A Complete Manual of Celestial Science, with Copious Illustra-
trations, Revised Calendar, Etc., very convenient for Clergy-
men's use (where people are still attached to existing forms of
worship) but more especially designed for Bishops (*Episcopoi*)
of the New Church *Perpetual*, and who will henceforth be "ob-
servers" of the Heavenly *times and seasons* as in the Ancient
Halcyon (Alcyone!) Salem- Shalom- or *Selah*-Days.

OTHER PUBLICATIONS:

(SOON READY)

THE "DOUBLE-W" [WW] MANIFEST!

Or the GENEALOGIES OF ISRAEL Disclosed. In Two
Volumes.

The Book of the Generations of WILLIAM PENN, (Kinghorn)
the Son of Joseph, (Ephraim) the Son of Israel.

The Book of the Generations of WILLIAM WALLACE, the Son
of David, the Son of Abraham. — And of all related to both
even to the tenth and twelfth degrees of Consanguinity.

"He was taken from *prison and from judgment* and who shall
declare his generation?"—*Isaiah*, 53 : 8.

And will *go again* if necessary in the defence of Truth!

But not trusting to the integrity of the **Law** or the magnanimity
of my enemies *I will declare My generation before I go!*

SELAH!

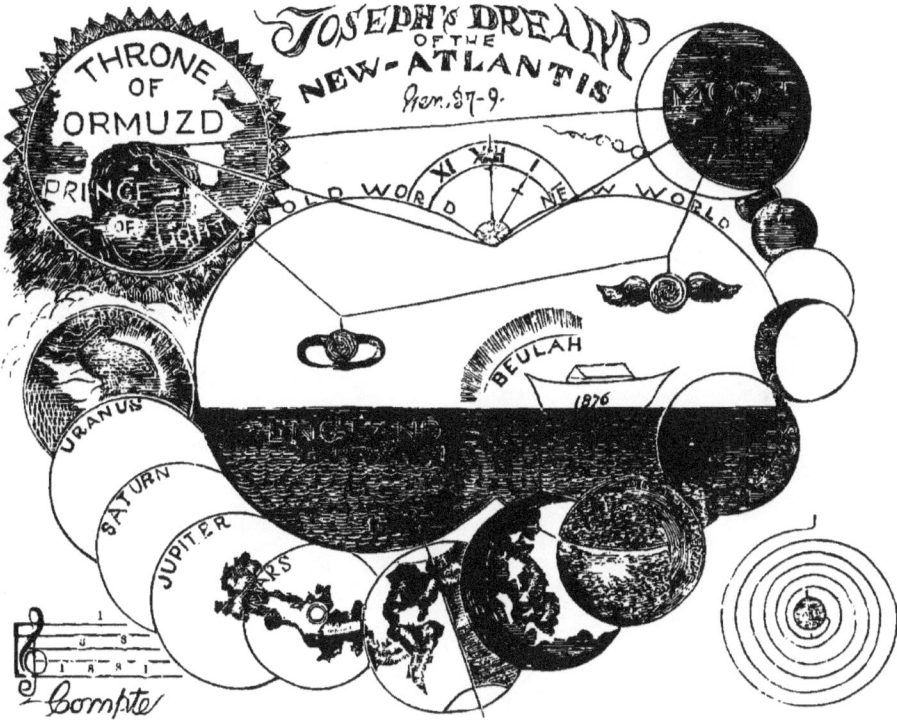

JOSEPH'S DREAM
OF THE
NEW-ATLANTIS
Gen. 37-9.

"Out of Egypt have I called My son."—*Esaias.*

BOOK II.
HERMES' HORNBOOK
FOR
BABES in JESHURUN
OR AN
INTRODUCTORY "FIRST-BOOK" TO A REVELATION OF THE
MYSTERIES OF THE WORD.

" As Moses lifted up the Serpent in the Wilderness even so must
this symbol of Hermetic Wisdom be lifted up."

BY

JOHN WALLACE JOSH-HORN,
(JESHURUN)
So named by his parents while " in Egypt."

HORNHOME PUBLICATIONS:
PHILADELPHIA.
1879.

A

INTRODUCTORY HINTS.

Would'st thou hear the Music of the spheres when the morning stars sang together, Approach, O thou who Canst, Lift the heart and withdraw the Veil!

Would'st thou know the Wisdom of the Egyptians, the secrets of Nirwana, and the Depths of the Magian Theosophy! Approach, O thou who Canst, Lift the heart and withdraw the Veil!

Look not for the Thunders of Sinai, nor the earthquakes in the path of Jeshurun, nor yet for the sword of the wrathful Mahmoud! for surely these things are of the Past, and unfit for the ushering in of the Reign of Peace!

Nevertheless, "Give a portion to Seven and also to Eight for thou knowest not what evil may be under the Sun."

Look not for the "end of the world" in the din and confusion of Yesterday and the still more blank uncertainty of To-day,—These are but the beginnings of time, and To-morrow but "a consummation of the Age."

Leave the Wrecks of the Past in the dust of Egypt, while we ascend to the New Zion "City of our God"—Approach O thou who Canst! Cover thy head, and withdraw the Veil!

Look at the worlds as they are evolved from Chaos, and roll majestically towards their Central Sun, and say if it is not that a new chord has been struck in the Harmony of the Universe, that the "times and dividing of times" has expired, and that the New Heavens and the New Earth have suddenly been revealed to man!

—Six stages of Earth are passed, and behold the Seventh!—"Let him that hath understanding count the number of the times, for it is the number of a man, and his number is Six hundred three score and Six."

Look at that Scale of the Shifting Worlds, and say if aught but the SOUL of Nature is imperishable! Forms are but the clay of the potter,—Types alone are Eternal!

Then say it thus with the Nations, in whom the Breath of the Deity has embodied the marching hosts of re-incarnate souls

37

for Armageddon's Conflict!—Let Truth survive, and dust return to dust!

KNOW THEN, O Man! that the time of that bloodless conflict is past, as the Israel of God returns from the Conquest of the Nations, bringing the fruits of victory and peace,—For the time for the "scattering of the Holy Seed" has been accomplished, and the "fulness of times" for their Return complete.

We are in the *Last Cycle* of Earth's whirling vortex of Waldensian Revolutions, O World, World, World!—the "wheel within wheel," the *Gilgal* of the Nations is at an end—Mars is out—Venus half-way through—and Mercury begun!

* * *   * * *   * * *   * * *

PROPHETIC RETROSPECT for the Year of Light, 11,250.

I stood upon the Earth in that latter day, and lo! a great noise as of a mighty earthquake! and a magnetic shudder thrilled through the Universe from centre to circumference, earth rose imponderable from her decayed and crumbling forms, sloughed her watery crust upon the surface of the Moon, took Venus as her satellite and thus equiped followed Mercury in his everlasting flight towards the centre of the Universe!!!

Given in the Spirit, on the Eve of the Transit of Venus, Dec. 8, 1874, and confided as a secret to Mr. Bp. Nick-elson, D. D. of the R. E. C., who has been gently breaking it to his Congregation, and others, recently, under the head of the "Gathering of Israel," now nearly four years since his enlightenment! Alas, poor Old Nick! if you had been Qu- C- Quick you would have divulged it sooner!

P. S.—As this goes to Press we are informed that the other factor of the R. E. C. Trinity "goes over" to see if the landing is all safe on the other side! Nov. 20, '78.

Bishop Cummins had failed to report.

How Quick they go! *lest somebody might be ahead of them in the resurrection.*

CANTERBURY HALL, 9th mo., '78, ⟩
    ☉ *in* ♐, *enciente of* N. C. E.! ⟨

38

BABEL UNBABBLED:

A
FEW
WORDS
FROM THE
HORNOGRAPHIC
DICTIONARY OF THE
CONFUSION OF TONGUES,

OR WORDS OCCURRING IN THIS WORK WHICH WERE ORIGIN-
ALLY THE SAME, AND ARE STILL OF SIMILAR MEANING

AARON, 'Arun, (*Sanskrit*) or Haran, or Charran, "calling,"
from Keren, (*Hebr.*) a Horn, Karen, keras (*Grk.*) "Heron, son-
of-Heron," or *Hermes*, (El)-Kurneh, or Karnak, Eg'pt'n. forms;
Ormuzd, Iran, *Airy'a'ne*, or Ariana, Aryan, Haranian or Iranian,—Persian synonyms. Indian or Brahminic form, 'Arun,
primitive.

Gos, Ges or Gesh, Gaash or Jesh, Geesh or Ghizeh, Gaza, the
Sun, Arun or Aaron, Son or child, horn or crown, Gesh-Arun
or JESHURUN, Geshur, Gos-horne or Goshen.

GAD, Gath or Goth, Gad-elians or Goths, from Gath or Gaza, "the Sun." Goths, Gotts, (*Ger.*) Gott, God, or "the Good."

Goths-spel or Goths' Word, Gottspel, or Gospel, Good Word.

Mary, Martha, Miriam, Maria, Meribah, *Bitterness.*

Gaul, gall, Algol, galal "to roll" Galilee, Gilgal, Goliah,
Gaulonite, Galatian.

PEN or Penn, Pem,(Horn or Peak) same as Pekah, "son of
Remaliah" (*Bible*), Leader of the Ten Tribes, or Samaritan Picts
or Ancient Scotch.

PENN, William of Pembroke, *Earl Jasper*, from Penuel,
"vision, or face of God" (see *Jacob*), Phineas, of the line of Aaron, Phenicians or Penn-icians.

Scots, *Scutii*, "shields" Scythians, *Cutheans* or Goths, bran-
ches of the Samaritan or more latterly Cathean Tribes.

39

Hebrides of the Heeb-rews, Heeb, "Hub" Il'o'p, or Hope, Ancient Welsh or Norse Discoverer of America and founder of the colony of Rhode Island. Mt. Hope.

JOB, Heeb or Hope, as in the hieroglyphics of Egypt a panegyric for the dead, "a hymn." Book of Job, an interesting relic of the Ancient Penn-ician Bible.

AZTECS, Aziatics:— Ah, A-az or Ahaz, Itz, Atz, Itzlan, Atlantic or *Atlanta*, the ancient submerged Atlantic or *Fortunate Isles*. Itz-Ra-El, or ISRÆL, "Soldier of God."

Æth, Ith, (see, Milesians in Spain) Athor or Æther, Venus or Isis, from Ath or Ith, the Moon.

Eth-i-'ope, (white) Man of the Moon, or *Man of Hope*.

Ethiopia, "land of Uz" the Ethiopic, or *Basic* Kingdom *of Job*, Iob, Heeb or Hope, the Adamic or Edom-ie basic kingdom of the Hebrews incorporated through patience and suffering into the Hierarchy of Salem or Jeshurun, Melchizedekian.

MAN, from "men" "to establish" — Menes, King of Upper Egypt (Ethiopia) Manes, Manx-man, (Isle of Man) Mohegan or Mexican, *Magian* (*Grk.* Magus or Ma-ke) Macedonian.

Salem, Shiloh, Silon, Salah, Sl am, Cœlum (heaven or haven) Selah, or *Salus*, Solace, Salmon, Shallum, Shulamite, (in Canticles), REST, Peace, or *Restoration*, or Shiloh, Union of the Church or the New Jerusalem with the Kingdom of Jeshurun. —(Solomon,—*Basic* imitation.)

Sheba, Queen of Arabia, or Seb, wife of Saturn, basic or imitative of Jeshurun or Israel. "Not all Israel that are *of Israel.*"

ZODIACK,— Zadok, Zedek or Sadoe, "*King Shaddai*," or Melchi-Zadok, King of Righteousness, or of Peace, Celestial, or Zodiakal. Cœlo-Syrians, Seleucidæ, and Sadducees.

Kadesh, "strife" Zadok, Zedek, *Peace*,—spelt backwards, or the Spirit of Strife as manifested at the "waters of Kadesh."

Angle-terre, *Angel-land*, Ingle-land, England or *Corner*-land. New Troy, Angle-*three*, and as triangular in shape as ever!

HORN-BOOK, Old English for *Primer*.

"Tohu-and-Bohu,"– Order and Chaos, Light and Darkness, "creating and uncreating," Upper and Lower (Egypt), creative and created *dynasties*, according to the Book of Ganesa, (Hindoo), Hebrew, or Greek, *Genesis*. (Deduced mainly from Egyptian Hieroglyphics, and more fully treated in another place.

Gansa, Gaza, Ghizeh, Gannet, "Goose," (the Sun), hieroglyphic. Canute, the Dane, Kenneth II, King of Scotland, 838 A. D., 69th in the direct line from Alexander the Great, of *Macedon*. Gaunt, John of Lancaster, *later*.

Geshe, Jeshe, Jesse, Jesus or Joshua, "the Sun," Jah or Jeshurun, or 'Arun "son of Jesse" or Son of the Sun, and from which as a patronymic was derived the Indo-Persian, Iranian or *Haranian* Kingdom of Salem, or that of Melchizedek, in the perpetual line of the Brahminic Priesthood, and which through the Covenant of Melchizedek with Abraham secures to the latter and to his seed forever the protection and favor of the King of Kings, and Lord of Lords, until they should be called home at the "consummation of the Age" as the New Israel to a kingdom "incorruptible, undefiled, and that fadeth not away."

GERSHON, or Gershom, "a stranger here" at the beginning of the Æon, or Age, was an appropriate designation for the son of Amram's (or, Amun-Ra) great grandsire, until his priestly line should in the "latter day" a second time lead up the hosts of Israel from the Ramesses of Egyptian Bondage to a Celestial Canaan, and though still *strangers here* "Of Haran are we!" and will leave this Land of Goshen which we do not want after the expiration of our *two* hundred year pilgrimage, and journey with the hosts of the New Israel towards our Haran home, or the *ancient* Hornhome, Land of the Orient.

HORNHOME, Haran, 'Arun or Aaron home, the Aaronia, Harania, Irania or the Persian *Airy'a'ne* or the Lost Eden of the Aruns, or Aryans or *Arians* or Karens of India, who under Canopus, "the Gannet" or, MaRabah Ganapata Goshain, son of the Sun, was the first leader of the Canopian, Ganapatian or Celestial host of Aryan world civilizers from the table lands of

India *through* Egypt to the plains of Iran or Haran, and the ancient Tyre or Troy.   Selah!

SELAH (City?) City of Love, from *Salus* "safety" salacious vigor of *Adonai*, or "Ich diene" "I serve" his Crest three ostrich feathers, and his ancestry from John of Bohemia, and Horn of Mount-Moriah-ney, (Montmorency) and William of Valentia (Pembroke or *Penn*).

> Now Prince of "Wails"
> Thou Prince of Tails!
> *It's HEADS I'll play tomorrow—*
> For Horn means "Crown"
> Of *London-town—*
> Then make your bed in *sorrow.*

> That "crown of pride" is Ephraim's still,
> By *George!* he will not borrow—
> But with his Wallace Broad-sword skill
> He'll crack your pow tomorrow!

> Then cease to trouble Israel's Rest
> With vain pretention's clamour:
> We've a Victoria in the West—
> C. Woodhull's awful glamour!

> This is the Dragon on our shores,
> From England's slimy bottoms,—
> And when we get some *datums* more
> *We'll finish up these thought-ems!*

FOWLER,– Phaula (Ger.) fol'wer or *imitator*, fallacious, or False Gemini, or Phallus, the *palsied* virile member.

In Genealogy, the teacher of false and corrupt principles from a degenerate virility; in Religion, a *mile away* (from Canterbury Hall) imitator of the Celestial Hornograph; in practice a sneak, or *snake*,–Infinitesimal attenuation of the *Tail of the Dragon!*

42

Origin, Pul or Phul, "a bean" a notoriously sickening vegetable coming up *bottom first* to the infinite disgust of all its respectable surrounding neighbors.

Ancestral and Phonetic, Phul, or *Fool*, or "*Free-knowledge-ist*" Free-lust, Phul-ist, from "phulla" (Grk.) "a leaf" first used in the Garden of Eden to cover the "shame" of *some* people's First Parents.

O my Tudor Princess, my Dove, my Church, my N. C. E.! my Lancastrian Gaunt, or Gannet, my own Petronilla Ale*Xan*-*drina* Lanfranc of Rhineland! how in times long past have I prayed with the Psalmist that the soul of my darling might be delivered from the "snare of the fowler!" and now that the late Transit of Mercury has given new power to the Son of the Sun, it becomes his unsavory duty to handle the "muck-rake" until from under the surface slums of this fair (?) City are disclosed the golden streets and pearly gates of the New Jerusalem! But *you* need not follow, O Xandrina! Let not curiosity, woman's besetting sin, tempt you to follow, but as you too with thy "sister" the Shulamite have sat under the ministrations, or otherwise been under the influence of the degenerate Shade of a degenerate sire, that Netherland curse of the House of Orange, *Vigilius de Quichem*, now more commonly known as the *Vigilant Old Quick* of R. E. C. notoriety, so I would have you put on your robes new-washed and sit a queen, and as fast as the New-born souls are delivered from "Quick and *Death*" I will send them in quiet pilgrimages to thy Canterbury shrine; and if there are those who say, Why does not the risen Lord cast off his erring and idolatrous (adulterous) "Church" *Let him 'hat is without sin among you cast the first stone at her!*

> For Enoch *Gershon* has returned
>   To be "a stranger here,"
> To find his long lost Arden home
>   Foul cursed at *Windermere*.

He halted not at Eden's Gate
  This sorrowing *Son of Man,*
But o'er the Sea at once he sped
  And this New World began!

* * *   * * *

Her heart still torn with grief and woe
  No consolation found,
Deceived, betrayed,
  She cursed the "spade"
  Her widowhood had found!

"I'll seek my lord and master still,
  Beyond the Sea' she said—
"Mayhap 'tis but an ugly dream,
  And Enoch is not dead!"

Translated! yes, O Father God,
  Thy sufferings now I see!
And those who "know" thy suffering Son
  Must find that One in—

  John, 10 : 30.

Hast thou never heard of HORNHOME, O thou dweller on this sin-cursed Earth! then hast thou yet to learn thy soul's First Lesson in the Book of Life! the very name and meaning of the HORNBOOK, not for "babes in Jesus" *now,* but for Babes in Jeshurun or the Son of Jesus (John) who again becomes the Father, as the Son of the Sun, and Sun of the Son, at this his "second coming" to draw his *Laiala* to him, and say "*We'll* have "a son" and we'll *hide him* in *Hornhome* till the wrath of Ahriman (Arrow-man) be past! And we'll call him Ormuzd or Hermes, and endow him with the Word of Life, and he shall be called in Heaven the Wonderful, the

44

Counsellor, the Prince of Peace, the Everlasting Father, to millions yet unborn, throughout all the starry worlds that tasted Adam's woe! My Laila, my Heart, my Love! *that Child is born!* We *sent* him, from Hornhome, but *not* from Christian street; 'twas *there* we met 'tis true, but *our* anointed was not to be a Christian, for he was born of no carnal thought, and no flesh and blood retards the winged Mercury in his flight of Light and Love through Fallen Worlds!

This is "Hornhome" O World, Aaronhome, Arnheim, Har-an-on-the-Rhine, where Cohorn Magi lit the fires of fading Orient to preserve the line of Salem's Seventh Son throughout its mighty conflict with Mediaeval Darkness and Ahriman's direst hate. And they said, *We'll* "hide him" through the mighty mysteries of our Ancestral Religion, that when the sword of Herod *Rome* shall seek his blood lest he appear at the head of Israel's Armies in the latter day, the Horn of Kyrnois (Corsica) shall wind the Marseillaise from the mountain fast-nesses of a *New* Hornhome, where the Orange-Nassau-renian "Kings of Holland" have for generations five nourished the soul of the Lion of Judah now glaring defiance from his Bohe-mian exile in Penn-Land to the wearer of his three ostrich feathers *across the Sea!*

FIRST PRIMER-LESSON.

"SHALL WE KNOW EACH OTHER *THERE!*"

Yes,— why not, when we pass over "Jordan!" Who wants a "mansion in the skies" when England's palatial residences are being emptied, swept and garnished in *momentary* prospect of their newly-found occupants, and Royal House of Hornhome (H. R. H.), H. B. M., S. S. S., IHS, I N R I, MM, WW, Etc., Etc., Etc.,!!! When the New Jerusalem "descends to Earth" shall we not be still more on *terra firma* than ever! and if we do not then meet our friends who have gone before woe to those who harp upon the words of the above song! they have no meaning! how can we come into our inheritance if we do not return to the homes whither our ancestral shades do call us?

45

"For here we have no abiding City but we seek one to come!"
Even Philadelphia is but the Goshen ("drawing near") of our
hopes, the "Beulah" of our wanderings! the last camping-place
west of the Jordan, that rolling, heaving, twisting, recoiling and
threatening Gulf Stream which represents the slimy coil of the
Zodiacal Dragon from under whose trail the "sweet influences"
of the Pleiades" and the *tightening* Bands of Orion are drawing
the submerged remains of the ancient continent of *Atlanta*, the
England of to-day, the long-lost Aryan-home of our pre-diluvian Ancestry! Our *Ancestors!* and where are they? Just
where they fell,—awaiting their re-entering into new and imperishable bodies that like Job they may stand *in their place* at
the latter day "in their flesh to see God" and the redemption
of Israel!

Then let the quartered remains of Sir William Wallace come
together on Tower Hill from the four *united* Kingdoms of
Great Britain, and with the blast of the Urus-horn assemble the
multitudes of Israel for the crowning of his son. Let another
Sir William (Penn) from the Burying-ground at Jordan's bring
his Tudor princess *Lilla* and say, Here is your "spirit-bride"
but of substantial flesh and blood, the *only* kind of *spirits* by
the way that this New Age will admit of, or are calculated to
do credit to the Resurrection of the Body. Take her for she
has waited long, and bears a Virgin name. 'Tis well; I 'll take
her, *for I know!* It's Rachel, this time, isn't it? Leah is lov-
ing, too, but you know you "promised" Rachel! Shall not the
Lion and the Lamb "lie down together" and be so docile that
"a little child" may lead them! if it is not so then I must be
mistaken in my Millennial reckonings, the world's Horoscope
will have to be re-cast and the two Celestial Signs, *Aries and
Leo*, which the *Little Gemini* now proclaims to be in harmony,
must be left out of the calculations altogether. Well, leave
them out then, O ye dull of understanding! and let this rocking
and reeling, and *wrecking* old world *go all to the bad*, for if the
Millennium is not here NOW when seven majestic planets roll
within conjunction limits before the next Transit of Venus in

46

1832 then will the writer of these "Hints" give up the Science of his forefathers, and say that That which has been is no longer that which shall be: for such Signs as the Heavens now unfold have never been seen without such certain results *since the world assumed its present shape!*

KNOW THEN! that

"OF HARAN ARE WE!"

And *WE*—are as follows:

From William the Silent to the younger son of the first of nine children—ten generations, five in the Westphalian provinces and five in Pennsylvania, bring a Golden Wedding in the Mountains of Pennland on the veritable *antipodal* spot where Jacob set up the stone of Pennel, and in that "vision of God" climbed the ladder which connected Earth and Heaven. Jacob or Israel, son of Rebekah of Haran marries Leah and Rachel, also of Haran, 1753 B. C., Jacob *Gershon* is born 1751 *the following year*, A. D.—twice fifty-two weeks of years or one hundred and four generations afterwards, involving one great cycle of time *as to Jacob's Line.*

Do you begin to get an inkling of a "Mystery" here, more profound than Babylon, O World! Then take out your "ear-cotton" and we will go on, and say, that from 'Arun, or Haran, son of Surya or Osiris, founder of the kingdom of Asher, 1771 B. C. (marriage), to Napoleon Bonaparte in *the following year*, 1769 A. D., twice fifty-four generations, or one hundred and eight in the line of the elementary principles, which brings us the Horn of Ganesa, "son of Siva," king-dethroner and annihilator of Papal bulls to say nothing of Dragons and other Apocalyptic monsters!

Collateral with this Line is the most ancient of all, the Chaldæan, Waldensian, Valentian, Gaulatian, Goliah-lan, Gaulonite, or Wallace-line, beginning far beyond the records of *his* history and *culminating* only in Scotland's champion broad-sword swinger, or if you choose his *lineal* descendent of just fourteen

generations in the maternal line, and could blow a resurrection
blast that would make the Prince (?) of Wal-es *wail* for the loss
of a kingdom *he never had* and has about as much claim to as
the little finger of the last of the descendents of the Tudors of
York and Lancaster! — But I am writing *History* now, not
raising the Dead,— unless he considers the Collateral of William and Mary as dead which all his Jesuitical counsellors will
hardly be able to reason into him! He's not a very bright
youth, *he* ain't! But perhaps he is hard of hearin' or *heard of
Haran!* and the proposed Transit of *Hermes!*

Is "Ancestry" my "hobby" think you? Well then, I'll
ride it *across the sea!* and when I wear my Ancestral Crown on
some bright Millennial morning I will begin *to complete* this
"Gilpin's ride" through the confusion of names and "tongues"
with which the Speech of the Earth is infected to the corruption
of morals, of doctrines, of history, of genealogy, of race, of *caste,*
of blood, of ANCESTRY, and in *consequence* of everything
that pertains to the welfare and harmonious developement of
the Human Race!

Hi! there! my Pegasus! (pege') Grk., or "Peggy" or *Mare,*
"sea" or *Mary,* and hence the whole story of the Roman Mother
and the Doge of Venice, or *Venus,* "marrying the Sea," and of
other still more venerable customs of which the Winged-Horse
is but the Celestial prototype and the personation of a principle
in Nature and *Man* which ceases not to act but with the end of
Time!

What a wonderful Language we have anyway! exactly corres-
pondent to the Celestial Signs and Constellations under which it
was developed, permeating like the liquid æther of Inspiration
through Nature's thousand-stringed and tuneful voice by which
as a creative power all things on earth are made according to
their pattern in the heavens, and no chord or syllable is lost to
all Eternity, but swells on in its fulness and grandeur as the
"Word" of God until the "fulness of times" when Heaven,
and Earth, and Sea are filled with the wonders of his name and

48

the glories of his power.

Hi! there! my Pegasus! my "hobby!" Speed on! Celestial "White-horse" until the clattering of thy iron hoof on England's shores strikes terror and dismay even where the pall of Death has so lately cast a foreshadowing gloom,—within "*Win-cer's!*" trembling walls! and the prince of *Wails* be compelled to nail a *horse-shoe* over his door as a talisman of safety and to propitiate—*not* the Horse and his Rider, O no! but the *Wrathful Lamb!* or *Aries*, England's "ruling Sign."

ISRAEL MUST RETURN!

If thou understandest not what thou readest then ask thy Neighbor, and if he cannot tell the meaning thereof let him ask his Minister, and let the minister tell it to the Church, and then let the Church invite the Author of the HORNBOOK to tell it to the ministers that the Ministers may tell it to the Congregation and the Congregation tell it to their neighbors, and thus the inquiring mind be satisfied.

THE NATIVITY.

Did I understand you to say that you had never heard of "Hornhome?" O World! Well, perhaps it is because of thy *limited education!* and will charitably lay it to the account of Mother Earth! But, Come, now! You have lost time enough! Open your "Hornbook" on First Page, and follow *the Pointer!*

HORNHOME, Nassau-earth,—from *nasci* "born" and *'aaretz* "earth" (later *Noss*-earth) Nativity 14th day of First Month, (not January) *year* of Mercury's *Prophetic* Transit, Wednesday, 11th Hour, Gemini ♊ Significator of the *Tu-dors* on the Meridian, Mercury ☿ (Lord the House) in Aries and approaching a Conjunction with the Sun ☉, *Regulus* in Leo ♌ rising in house of Conception, ♌ and in Conjunction with Luna ☽ *Significatrix* of the *Church!* and indicative of success in Her search for a very *promising* Youth! See Canticles *in loco.*

BylineageaNazarenebornintheNewGalileeoftheGentilesofreligion sbut*respectable*parents-fitoriginforthenewcarpentersson "Joseph"

Lillie!   &   *Lizzie!*

"TWO–DOORS"

TO THE "MANY MANSIONS."

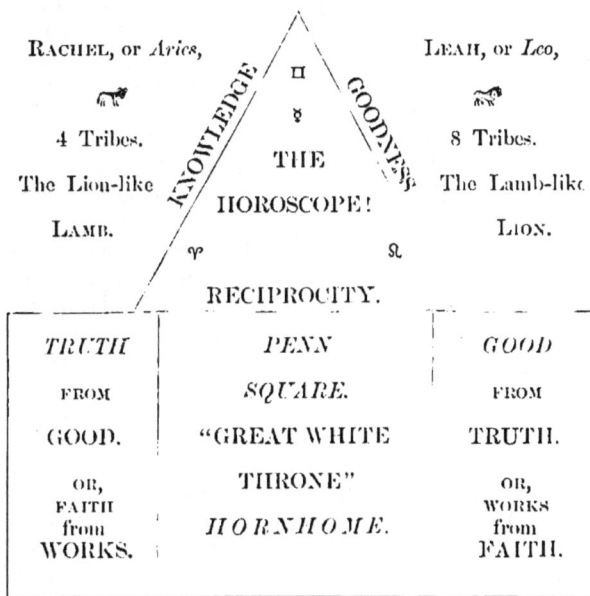

RACHEL, or *Aries*,   LEAH, or *Leo*,

4 Tribes.   THE   8 Tribes.

The Lion-like   HOROSCOPE!   The Lamb-like

LAMB.   LION.

(KNOWLEDGE   GOODNESS)

RECIPROCITY.

TRUTH	*PENN*	*GOOD*
FROM	*SQUARE.*	FROM
GOOD.	"GREAT WHITE	TRUTH.
OR, FAITH from WORKS.	THRONE" *HORNHOME.*	OR, WORKS from FAITH.

EASTWARD, HO!

"CANTERBURY HALL,"   MOODY-AND-SANKEY

New Church Episcopal.   *DEPOT.*

N. W. Cor.   S. W. Cor.

13th & Market.   13th & Market.

ROYAL HOUSE OF HORNHOME;

OR THE

"CHURCH IN PHILADELPHIA"

Rev. 3 : 7.

"CANTERBURY PILGRIMS."

THIS way! O thou Traveler over Life's dusty Road! *This* is the Way to the Eternal City! and at one or the other of these "Two-doors" must thou enter, if thou enter at all, into Israel's Rest! "Jachin" and "Boaz" those Pillars of the Ancient Temple now support the Right and Left "wings" of the "Church in Philadelphia" first and principal of all the Seven, and flourishing now into a glorious immortality! Gather here, O Israel, at this the advent of thy Fiftieth Jubilee, fifty-times-fifty years from the Captivity! That is a long time to wait for thy redemption from *spiritual* bondage! *but it has come at last!* Return ye now to a *New* Jerusalem, O ye Dispersed of Israel! Are Judea's arid plains and sun-scorched hills a more inviting prospect than the undulating vales of green Old England! Has not Palestine itself shifted westward with the Precession of the Equinoxes, and the Star which guided the Magi *two thousand* years ago to the secluded Nativity of the "Horn-Child" now rests serenely in the Zenith of our Western World! Be quiet *Wester-reldt*, I am not ready yet to deal with the awful mystery of thy incarceration: but one would think the blood of the Ross-horn would not only "wash away" the guilt of the parents, and all those concerned in the secret propagation of the Red-Line Stuart Pretendership which by some strange fatality has had *seven heads* cut off in as many hundred years since Baliol or *Be-lial*, foe of Bruce and Wallace, from being the King's scullion was made a Chief *Stuard* of the realm of Scotland, but would throw open the prison-doors of Moyamensing and set free the *unfortunate* partner in a perfidious plot! It is but fitting that the Reign of Mystery and the Scarlet Woman should close its career of blood and Superstition and *Sorcery* by *another* Mystery (?) of a Bethlehem *Baby*-lon concocted full *five years* too soon to mark the *birth* of the New Era in 1881, just as *that other* grandest farce ever produced on this stage of action was enacted precisely the same length of time before the beginning of a former *New Era* when John the Nazarene "began to be about thirty years of age" *and mighty works began to show forth them-*

51

selves in him!

Now that the time has come for the Christ and the Anti-Christ to contend again for the throne of their ancestors, God and the Devil, the Minister-General will just call out a few detachments of Hornhome troops who may be reconnoitering the Field of Armageddon while the idolizers of the "Stuart Pretender" and his bastard issue throng in babbling crowds to the cry of "Wha'll be King but Charlie?" only to be *swept* from the field by the truer hearts and stronger arms which rally to the border-slogan of "Scots wha hae wi' Wallace bled!"

Napoleon to the RIGHT! Bear up the Charlemagne Crown of Orange! Wallace to the LEFT! Support the *Son of David*, and Scotia's Ancestral Kingly Line! There! The Crown of England, the Great Koh-i Nor Diamond in London Tower, (or the "white-stone" of Revelations) and the Redemption of Israel is the Prize!

PREPARE FOR THE ONSET!

"*The Kings of the Earth set themselves, and the Rulers take counsel together—against the Lord, and against his Anointed!*"

Then sound the *Marseillaise* until that great intervening *Jordan* shall *hiss* with the blood of Israel's accursed foes: for more Kings have been dethroned at that Battle Hymn of the martial hosts of Heaven than by any other cry that ever rent the empyrean vault since the "*Ua-la-la! la-la!*" *Vwala*, or *Wallace!* war-whoop of the Spartans strewed many a Marathon with the trophies of Victory and Death!

But halt—STAND!

THE ARGUMENT!

"Peradventure there be *but one* righteous person among all these faithless *Stuards!* wilt thou destroy the City for lack of more?" (Gen. 18:32.)   *The Father of Nations pleads.*

Angry Son.—"I am not come to send Peace on earth but a Sword!"

The Father.—"But the Heathen are thine *inheritance*, and the uttermost parts of the Earth thy *possession.*"

52

Son. But their cry is "This is the heir, Come, let us kill him and the Vineyard shall be ours!"

The Spirit. (Admonitory,) " *Kiss the Son lest he be angry and ye perish from the way when his anger is kindled but a little.*")

Father. "Behold the Tabernacle of God is *with men.*" And as for this " *Eleazar of Damascus*" called "mine heir" he shall no longer be *Stuard* of mine house!

Son. Ah! the doom of the Stewart Line so long ago as that! Surely, Creation must be a stupendous joke! *Let us return to Pre-Adamite principles?* Creation is much older than is commonly supposed! Is it not?

Father. Not so old *by half* since in Abraham was created a "world from nothing" and Isaac or "laughter" was the *prom-ise* that by this "stupendous joke" "all the Nations of the Earth should be blessed!"

Son. And Esau or "anger" or *Adam* was an *afterthought* of God's, and no part of the original Divine Plan?

Father It *need not* to have been but *was.*

Son. Then we had need to go still farther back than Adam, or than "Father Abraham" for the cause of Sin or the origin of Evil in the world?

Father. You need go no farther than your own individual life to solve the "Mystery" that has draped the world with sin and woe.

Son. I had nothing to do with the Ross-Mystery.

Father. You founded the line of the Pretender by an illicit connection with the Daughters of Men.

Son. As whom? '

Father. As Joseph—when in Egypt you married *Asenath,* a daughter of Potiphera, priest of On, instead of seeking for thy *ancestral* spirit among thy Haran kindred.

Joseph. As *Egypt* still represents the "world" and *I* the spi-rit of Man in bondage thereto,—

Father. —You would perpetuate that bondage by another marriage with a daughter of the King's *Stuard!*

Joseph. But I am still in Egypt—or in bondage to the flesh!

Father. "Out of Egypt have I called my Son!"

Joseph. That saying is applied by the Babylonians to Joseph the Carpenter's son!

Melchizedek. But was rather intended for you as the *Carpenter's son Joseph* at his final appearing.

John. That is still my father's profession though by birthright Lord of the Isles of Bute and *Ha*-ran.

Melchizedek. And would have been King of Free Scotland in the right of his wife had it not been for an illicit blending of the rising line of Wallace with that of Stuart through the Earls of *Ross* and Mar.

Angry SON.—Then Hel-en Mar has marred my genealogy *like HELL!!*

"*Malcom-of-Zadok.*" Patience! My Son! the *Curse is out!*

Earl David's-Son of Huntingdon.— Yes "out" on *dress parade!* in the vain confidence of an Armageddon Victory!

Malcom. That is Apollyon's way—a blustering braggadocia to frighten tender-hearted saints into the idea that the sword of Amalek still guards the exit from the Wilderness, and that their promised inheritance is about to be trodden under foot!

Crown Prince of Goshen. Is that the language of the Prince of Wales!

Malcom-Zedek. If he were capable of speaking it.

Shiloh. But "it would be a pity" to dethrone Hohenzollern?

St. George. Not if you will exalt Hesse-*Casshel!*

Shiloh. Ah! My Rhineland Princess! *Wohl-geboren?*

George I. Yes!—*well-born* but not —*Wolbert!*

Poor Artist. Not my 'ittie 'illie 'olbie! with the Auburn hair and German lisp?

54

George II. Not your "little" Lillie Wolbert—you made her so proud of her expected Coronet that she *wouldn't speak to you* till you should be *King of England!*

Crown Prince. That *didn't hurry me any!* for I only took a three years *vacation* and *then* didn't return *to her!*

George III. You always had exalted ideas of retributive justice, but what will you do if Rachel should be *restored* to you after you have espoused Leah?

Jacob. I shall *take both!* as formerly and thus fulfill my destiny as the Father of Israel!

George the Last. Then you are no longer the Son when all crowns and kingdoms are subject to the one Central throne of England, as a thousand years ago prefigured in the Saxon Heptarchy when the Seven kingdoms of Salem's Seventh Son were united under the sceptre of the Ephraimite, that around that standard of the Son of Joseph might gather for a thousand years longer the Dispersed of Israel in anticipation of the "fulness of times" when the prophetic Shiloh should break the bonds of his long imprisonment in kingly genealogies and speak the Word as one having authority *and not as the Scribes!*

Then Disperse! Ye Rebels against the Divine Law of Love and Harmony! *we'll have no Armageddon!*—but will inaugurate Earth's Great Peace Jubilee, or the Seventh Millennial nuptials of *Har-*anos and *Geesh* ('ouranos and gēs) or the New Heavens and the New Earth *in Jeshurun,* by one of Nature's touches "which makes the whole world kin" on the Fourteenth Day of the First Month (February) still presided over by the patron saint of *Valentia* or *Wales,* or David's Son *St. Wallace,* since now "the child is father of the man" in a different sense from what is commonly understood, and from being Crown Prince of Wallace now becomes *Regent* of the dominions of his father David, and with his chosen one is his own Father and his own Son, For

OF *HEAVEN* (Hauran) ARE WE!

O Earth! (Gos)

And this

Marriage of Earth and Heaven once solemnized by the Sun and
Moon at the Old Old Mohegan Home at Goshen in the Connec-
ticut Valley in the days of the Pre-Diluvian Israel now mani-
fests the perpetual *re*-generation of the Son-of-the-Sun, Creation's ever-recurring New-Birth in the two-fold unity of the
Divine Humanity of the Son of Man!

Note, O World! that in our voyaging through space we have
struck the Arc of *Cephas* and the boundaries of Taurus, or Terra (Earth) or the "House of Joseph" "from whence is the
Shepherd the *New White Stone* of Israel." Gen. 49 : 24, Rev. 2 :
17.

Study Astronomy and your Bibles will be more serviceable.

But here comes my *Steward* Princess, the *Elect* Xandrina (Al-
exandrina) Scotia's *Russian* Princess! hidden near the later ancestral home of the Horn-child at Arnheim on the Rhine, and
without peradventure that *only* one for whose sake I will not destroy the whole *Stuard* line, but all their crimes shall be remit-
ted to them for *her sake* and only at the cost of a pilgrimage to
her Canterbury Shrine! Enough of the Stuart blood has been
shed in the oft-repeated but vain attempt to place the *Pretender*
upon the throne to *wash away their own sins*, and that category
is as long as the Line itself and as varied as the multitudinous
family names that would still rally at the elevation of the standard of that *heir*-less Cause now mute forever in the inglorious
dust! The head of the "Chief-Baker" has again been lifted
from the shoulders *of his son!* and the "Chief-Butler" is again
restored to his *Steward*-ship of the King's household in the person of his Elizabethan daughter,—*and the divining-cup of Joseph
is as reliable as ever!*

I'm through! O World! Never mind how I got here, or if
curious consult Pythagoras on *re-incarnation*, or Plato on the
New-Birth of the Soul, or John on the Resurrection of the
Body and the Advent of *Rabbi Ben Israel.* HERE I AM! "in
the clouds?" as the Babylonians are probably asking,— yes, *in
the clouds!* Oh ye Christianized Worldlings, unless you see me a
great deal more plain'y than I think you do! What matters it

56

whether I come *down* from Hell, or UP from Heaven! I've been through BOTH! "*Out of Egypt* have I called my *Son*," that is, my inner or spiritual self. Joseph is *his own* father, and when you solve the Sphynx Riddle of how

I and my Father are my brother's Son,

Then will you know how *we three are one!*

Brother *David*, you're a "brick!" I believe that is what they called *Laban*, according to the *Bible Dictionaries* at all events! Then, since *thou art my son!* ("this day have I begotten thee") ("For if thou call'st me *Lord*, how then am I *thy* son?") then will "I give thee *England* for thine inheritance, and the uttermost parts of the Earth for thy possession!" Am I not still the younger son, from everlasting to everlasting the Immortal Youth, without father or mother in the spiritual sense, and him whose genealogy is not counted from Abraham, nor yet *from Adam*, and of what avail to me are all the honors and titles of this world which now as in the beginning I have only *made out* for the encouragement of my earth-born son or older brother, whether as Cain, or *King*, or Esau, *Earth*, or *David*, still improving at every new incarnation as the earth-man into a better disposition towards thy younger or spiritual brother, who now as the latest born and more enduring as *Joseph the fruitful bough* becomes the Lord and Giver of Life to new scions and their *parent stem!* and as from *him* was to come forth "the Shepherd the *Stone* of Israel" it is easy to be seen how I might still deprive Edom of his birth-right by a marriage with the *two Princesses*, daughters of Laban or *Haran*, offshoots of my *ancient* elder-brother's line, and again become my *brother's father*, with the *three crowns* of England all my own! And *Jacob* will probably marry!

Are we *verging on mysteries*, O World? Well then perhaps I had better stop! lest I may be misunderstood! and take more time and leisure as *King of England* to interpret the meaning of those *Six Books* which I wrote while in Egypt, and only *stopped short* because the world's *Seventh* Millenary, or the time for the breaking of the *Seventh Seal* by the Seventh Son of David who was the Seventh Son of Jesse, or *Geshe*, of *Haran*, had not yet arrived, and the consequent difficulty of the Son of the Sun's explaining how as *Haran of Geshe* or the Horn of David he came to be *his own and elder-brother's father* was doubly enhanced!

But I was going to England *with my three crowns!* Shall I go? *Sir* Thomas Carlyle, you have been awaiting me long, and you are the only man in England fitted either by birth or education to confer the Crown: Like Samuel of old prepare for the anointing of *my little David*, first-born because the last-born and at present attending his *pastoral* flocks in the fertile meadow lands of Western Virginia, all unconscious of the crown of Charlemagne now a thousand years maturing for his brow, and *Carl*-isle, the *prophetic* man, shall be his Lord-Keeper of the Privy Seal! Never mind the *ignoble* "Nobility" of England, their titles *wont wash!* and they are sadly in need of it! O that the Gulf-Stream, that silent Minister of the Almighty *Will*, would *vicariously* atone for England's regicidal sins, and, from creeping gently around her sinking shores, heed the Galactic Jordan-swell and give that old Atlantidæan Isle *another* gentle "swash!"

But, Brother! you have come to see me go! That's *nobly* done, and like a noble brother! You wait the parting word, the last Adieu! The "All-aboard!" has sounded from the Zion Ship. I go! What! Thou *David*-born, and named, and thus resign a crown? Ay, worthy thou of *son*-ship now: "*This day have I begotten thee!*"

My Son or *brother* David! was it not written: Ephraim shall not envy Judah, and Judah shall not vex Ephraim? then is that this day fulfilled. "King Orion's" Starry Realms *should* be enough for me,—but what does Jacob say! "The Sceptre shall not depart from Judah nor a Law-Giver from between his feet, till *Shiloh* come!" Shiloh *has* come! but I'll *improve on Jacob* and will not *supplant my brother!* Earth's sceptre's Judah's still! Here! *Take it!* brother, for to rule is *weariness to me!* But since the Gulf-Stream's old-time Atlantidæan swell now *Eastward* rolls we'll just stay on *this side* of the water *and let Old England take another plunge! * * ***

"*THE NEW HEAVENS AND THE NEW EARTH!*"

OR

THE NEW ATLANTIS.

Submerged 8000——4000, A. M. Restored—*at the same rate of speed that England is sinking year by year!* Discovered by the Northmen (Returning *Atlantides*) about 800, A. D. *Re*-discovered by Columbus 1492. Its *Central Province* Chartered by Penn, March 4th 16-81. Bi-Centenary, or Penn-Jubilee Inauguration, March 4th, 1881.

Behold! "I am *ready to be offered*," but not to the Presidency! I'll *improve* on Dr. Watts:

> *Judah* shall reign where' er the *Son*
> Does his *successful* journeys run,
> *His* kingdom stretch from shore to shore
> Till *Norman brats* * shall vex no more!

> To *Ephraim* let your *prayers be made!*
> Let "*Fox*- * tail" trophies crown his head,—
> 'Tis *Joseph's son* that *dies for* thee!
> And hunts the *dam Norway rat from sea to sea!*

There! O World! Shall I "punch him" now! Or what is the use of "plugging" the Old Ship of Zion for another voyage if that *dam* "varmint" is to be left inside? *Paul* him out there, that corrupter of New Testament Theology *and still alive* in the *descendents* of that "queer" old *bachelor!* What a "funny" world this is anyway when a *P*(a)*nd-in-e* "ubiqui-tress" enters one of the *very* largest mercantile establishments in Our City,

---

* For more complete understanding of these allusions, *See* further "*Hints*," etc.

armed with "Inhalers" (*in-hell-ers*) for *both ends*, and acts as *procuress* (for a certain *nameless* physician) among the many unsuspecting damsels domiciliated there! and with the purpose (as fast as they are successfully *treated* and demoralized by these two twin-medical *vampires*) of replenishing therewith the depleted ranks of *Shakerism!* There! O World! Ephraim is a little out of breath with that *hunt* but he'll *shake her* for all that, "the *varmint!*" until her "spirit-children" will still more than usual *hardly recognize their quon-dam mother!*

But since we have very little time to deal with the *Paul Prys* of Society, and the work of "the Ephraimite" among the "*small fry*" of Paul the "little," or *Saul* (sheol) "hell" draws near its close I would simply remark to those who may as yet be unacquainted with the origin and *fatal significance* of certain family-*names*, the family *traits* of those who perpetuate their name in the world by what they choose to term "spiritual-children" are as *ineradicable* now in certain characters who continue to call forth that cry from Heaven of the vilified and outraged *Nazarene:* "Paul! *Fool!* Why persecutest thou Me?

'Tis hard to *kick against the pricks!*"
Because you have no prong!

Then let *Adonai* alone, with his loves! He knows your *infirmity*, and when you submit yourself to the great Soul-Physician he will cure it and then at some future time it may find a body more suitable through which to perform its functions. But *do* not attempt to pass from the *Gentile* division of the Benjamite family to the *right-hand* inheritance of that other branch, whose *name* and deeds *of course* show them, wherever found, as worthy their inheritance among the other members of the great Family of Israel. There is the *bar sinister* and it is impossible, and all the *Jeshurun* blood shed by Paul the Benjamite and his great prototype Saul the *Benjamite*, the persecutor of David, cannot *wash out* the guilt of those "left-handed slingers of Benjamin" who to this day *persecute* because they cannot *rule* the "children of light," nor use the "divining-cup" of Joseph the Hebrew which *was found* in "Benjamin's sack" without in

60

their ignorance and spiritual witch-*craftiness* degenerating into all the *Fox-*y delusions of Modern-Quake-Shakerism!

Then do not think to pass that *left bar* to the Kingdom of Light and Honor without submitting like the *original* Paul to be purged *by lightning* from moral and physical impurity as the *laws of regeneration* require before you can even be considered *immortal* much less as fit to take your seat at the *right hand* or among the *Nobility* of the New Israel. And *such* regeneration would require an Age at least to accomplish!

Speaking of Shakers reminds me of *Shak-spear*, and Shakspeare reminds me of a *fool*, and a Fool reminds me of *Solomon!* *another Benjamite* Franklin who stole "fire from Heaven" in the wisdom of *Haran* King of Tyre, as Shakspeare *bottled* Lord Bacon's *Wisdom of the Ancients*, or as *Granny Franklin* ketch't lightnin' to every school-boy's eulogistic astonishment ever since, an *innocent* pastime of the Great *Juggler* compared with his *jug*-ging the Wisdom of Mother Goose, or scribbling libels on William Penn, or filching away the property of his heirs, or even "coming back" as the Father of Modern Spiritualism and whispering through the white lips of the *Fox-*Girls that rallying name of *hope* for all the *Luciferians* in Hell, *Charles B. Ros-ma!* the very name of Captain Kid-*nab*'s Philadelphia *Prince*—the last 'lorn hope of *the Belial Pretender*—the last wailing note of the *Dead March in Saul!*

Now *Judah*, if you think you can keep the "little Foxes" and other "varmint" "which spoil the vines" out of your dominions, Ephraim will put up his *shootin'-stick* for awhile, nor will *zhe leetle Sham-son* tie any more of their tails together as he did those *twin-physicians'* (male and female *tied he them*) and set them loose to spread consternation among the *Paulis*tians whose goings forth are from *Vineland* to the uttermost parts of the earth!

And thou, too, O world, when thou wouldest be reminded of how long and faithfully the *Eternal Fool* has reigned under the *Son*, and been considered *wise*, read the proverbs of Solomon, the puerilities of Socrates, the twaddling rhymes of Lord Bacon's *footman*, the insipid plagiarisms of Benjamin Franklin, and then to conclude all, turn to that *last effort* of his even from *Limbo* to "reform the world" the result of which is *feelingly* expressed in the following

EPITAPH!

HERE *LIES*

MODERN SPIRITUALISM!

When it says
it was not born on

"ALL-FOOLS' DAY"

[April 1st.]

Of the Virgin (Fox-Girls), or *hidden* at Hydesville, New York, [See History of the *Rochester-Knockings*] (some distance from where "Ephraim" afterwards *hided* him!) Ben. Franklin Chief Agitator, and *Reinecke Fuchs* General Contriver of "blue-light" pyrotechnics in that last attempt of the *Luciferians* to "put out the Son" so that their infernal "dark-circles" might everlastingly be uninterrupted!

DIED!

Of a Paralytic Stroke of

CONDENSED LIGHTNING

After a *lingering illness* contracted from EXPOSURE of "Katie King" at the "funeral" of that hope of the *Lewis-fers*, Chas. B. Ross-ester, in that dreary winter (for fraudulent practices) of '74.

And though ceaselessly prating of Immortality, now to be *buried beyond the hope of a Resurrection!*

Friends, Relatives, and *Dupes*, to the extent of *one-third of the human race* (Rev. 12:4) are requested to meet at the late residence of the deceased (so-called "Washington Family") 15th and Oxford—wheretotheastonishmentofall"ginooineinvestigators"itwillbeburiedsecretlyin

THE BACK YARD!

&

here
ends
the
Tail
of the
Dragon
which
"drew down
the third part
of the stars of
heaven and cast
them to the earth,"
whose Body is in Eng-
land, whose Heart is in
Rome, and whose Head is
in *Babylon*, where by the "Confusion of Tongues" or the *corrupting
of language*, it gained an ascendancy over
the pure principles of the *Hermetic Philosophy*, which from the time of Joseph the Hebrew
until the Decline in Solomon had filled Egypt
with its Monuments, Tyre or *Troy* with its
Splendors, and Jerusalem with the dying efful-
gence   of PERSIA's Ancestral, Celestial,   *Haranian*   Fires! which were kindled by   "Adon"
ere *Adam*   had a name, whose Fall is   now redeemed
by this "wounding" of the Head of the
dragon which the *Unsealing* of the
NEXT of the *Hermetic Books*
will knock *all to
damn smash!*
A
B   R
R   B
A   A
C   D
A   A
D   C
A   A
B   R
R   B
A B R A C A D A B R A

REFLECTIONS!

By Ecclesiastes, or The Preacher;
"new church episcopal."

I, the Shiloh-Man, was King of Israel in the Ancient City of *Phylae,* before there was any King of the Jews at *Jebus,* and instead of penning "wise sayings" or Proverbs that no sensible person can understand, or that a *Fool* might understand *without* being told, I set myself vigorously to work to solve the mystery of Human existence, and then afterwards to destroy the mischief-makers of Society which undermine the peace and prosperity of the *New* Salem, by a prolonged siege of "hunting-and-trapping" that with the exception of the Labors of Hercules, has perhaps been unparalleled in the History of Man!

And I said to my Heart, Behold I have already seen many days in which there has been naught but vanity and vexation of spirit: for thou seest that "but one thing happeneth to the wise man and the fool" except that the days of the fool are prolonged to an unreasonable length, while the wise man is as often "taken from the evil that is to be" much sooner than he cares to be relieved from that gloomy prospect.

And my Heart said, Get wisdom and seek after understanding, and that which thou now considerest as a gross perversion of justice will in the end be deemed by you to be the sublimest "joke" ever perpetrated by the Creator upon suffering Humanity.

And I did so, and we explained it together in this way, that the worst and the *best* of Life consisted in this,

"That the fools and wicked, with their master Satan, do confidently hope that in the End of the conflict for the dominion of the world that they will be successful, and at the last to find themselves overthrown with an everlasting and inglorious defeat.

"While on the other hand, the wise and good of all times and ages have been in constant dread of annihilation by the Powers of Darkness, yet in reality have been victorious at every point, and in the End have worsted the Devil beyond their most *sanguinary* expectations."

64

And I said, As this is so, *and I have lived to see it!* I will
say no more about "vanity and vexation of spirit" unless for-
sooth it is to be *made out* that "there is no Hell" for these wolf-
ish Benjamites and others to go to, and then will the Heart
of the "poor Ephraimite" *Preacher* be oppressed indeed! For
though Beecher, the *Bachrite*, another *son of Benjamin* may be
excused for declaring when he *touched bottom* that there was *no
hell there!* yet the afterclap might have revealed *even to one of
his experience* that stolen lightning *burns at last!*

And I said to my Heart of this Great Preacher, or Son of
Solomon, that I *did not think he was such a fool!* For as the
"son of the right hand" I had built great expectations upon
him. But as the "son of" the right hand according to the system of Hermes always *goes to the left*, so Beecher has been true
to his destiny as the Bacch-ite, the King's Chief-Butler, Cup-
bearer or *Steward*, and who has this one redeeming quality
above all the other Benjamites herein alluded to, that he does
his own thinking and does not live *by filching other peoples'
brains!*

Then, be a faithful steward of the mysteries which are shortly
to be revealed unto thee, but to which thou wast not *born*, or
you never would have cursed your little *Ham-son* (by calling
him a "Boston-mulatto" or something,) just because he was
white enough to expose the miscegenation practices in the tent of
Noah, which Shem and Jap. tried to cover with a blanket. I
appeal from Bacchus *drunk* to Bacchus sober: *which* was the
most worthy of your indiscriminate vituperation?

Then we will dispense with the drinking-cup, and with the
butler of course, lest the "spiritual manifestations" which it
produces among congregations *sacramentally* as well as in private *circles* may beget another spawn of the Lernean Hydra
like that which so recently begrimed the waters of regeneration
that the *Stuard Princess* Xandro-meda could scarcely pass the
T. Benjamin Wat(ch)ford with her *Perseus* deliverer without
being besmirched with his maudlin—*clash!*

And moreover, I said to my heart, the Harp of Troy, or
Tara, has long been mute, since in the Halls of Terah, *before*

Abraham was, we touched its chords of a thousand songs to the Æolian strains of a far-off Celestial Harmony: can we not together from our mutual consciousness restore a few of these lost notes of the world's forgotten melodies, and have them lisped to *the Transit Scale* wherever the English Language is spoken, while the walls of that Temple which was made without hands again shall rise with the submerged Atlanta, and from this Sunset Land evolve the New-World of Letters and of Song! And my Heart said, Yes! your head is for thought, and your heart is for song and now that *Aries* and *Leo* approach their final and harmonious conjunction the key-note of the New Song of Moses (?) and the *Lamb* has been struck to-day (St. Valentine's) for the first time since "the morning stars sang together and all the Sons of God shouted for joy!" Yes, *said I,* and the "bones of Joseph," with the *buried Wisdom of Hermes,* shall be together "carried up *out of Egypt*" at this the 99th 33 year Transit of Mercury since the Exodus, and the 70 years till 1879, and from the elevation under Alexander 333 B. C. the 66th (Transit) and from the first opening up of the Foreshadowed Land of Joseph's Dream by the Norse discoverers of this Western Land of Promise, the 33rd! that last turn of the "wheel" of human destiny, the loosening of the "silver cord" and the breaking of the "golden bowl," when all life shall return to him who gave it, as one Transit of Mercury as the Lord and Giver of Life just precisely compasses one generation of men, and as one generation cometh another goeth, and as Israel returns to her pre-diluvian habitation the lips of the Preacher pronounce that watchword of the New Era which was death for a Roman Citizen to utter:

"*VALENTIA!*"

For the conclusion of this work refer to the Introduction, and from the introduction again to the Conclusion: For the NEW TIARA is the *Tarrot* solved, and "Truth's" beginning is the end of MYSTERY!

$$666 \ \square \ 4 = 2664, \text{ A. U. C.} = \text{Rev. } 13:18.$$

RETURN! RETURN! RETURN!
O ISRAEL, RETURN!

www.ingramcontent.com/pod-product-compliance
Lightning Source LLC
Chambersburg PA
CBHW021513090426
42739CB00007B/585